WEDNESDAYS WITH JAMES

Coaching

a guide for beginners

Copyright © 2024 by Wednesdays with James

All rights reserved. No part of this publication may be reproduced, stored or transmitted in any form or by any means, electronic, mechanical, photocopying, recording, scanning, or otherwise without written permission from the publisher. It is illegal to copy this book, post it to a website, or distribute it by any other means without permission.

First edition

*This book was professionally typeset on Reedsy.
Find out more at reedsy.com*

Contents

1 Introduction TO COACHING	1
The benefits of coaching are multifaceted:	2
2 Understanding the Coachee	5
1. Understanding the Coachee	5
2. Establishing the Coaching Agreement	6
3. Preparing the Coaching Environment	6
4. Self-Preparation of the Coach	7
5. Utilizing Assessment Tools	8
3 Activity	9
Coaching Needs Questionnaire	9
4 Structuring Effective Coaching Sessions	13
1. Introduction and Rapport Building (5-10 minutes)	13
2. Review of Previous Actions and Progress (10-15 minutes)	14
3. Setting the Session's Objective (5-10 minutes)	14
4. Exploration and Insight Development (20-30 minutes)	14
5. Action Planning (10-15 minutes)	15
6. Summary and Closing (5 minutes)	15
5 Implementing Effective Coaching Techniques and Tools	19
1. The Wheel of Life	19
2. SMART Goal Setting	19
3. Journaling Exercises	20

4. Mindfulness and Centering Techniques	20
5. Powerful Questioning	20
6 Reflection and Feedback in the Coaching Process	26
1.Encouraging Self-Reflection	26
2. Providing Constructive Feedback	26
3. Seeking Feedback as a Coach	27
7 Contact Us.	32
8 References	34

1

Introduction TO COACHING

Coaching is a collaborative and transformative process designed to help individuals unlock their potential, overcome challenges, and achieve personal or professional goals. At its core, coaching is not about providing direct answers but empowering coachees to discover solutions, develop new skills, and grow in ways that are meaningful to them.

As Sir John Whitmore, a pioneer in the field, stated, "Coaching is unlocking a person's potential to maximize their growth."

The purpose of coaching is to foster self-awareness and personal agency. Whether navigating career transitions, enhancing leadership capabilities, improving performance, or finding work-life balance, coaching provides the tools and support to move forward with confidence and clarity.

Renowned coach Bill McCartney encapsulated this by saying, "All coaching is, is taking a player where he can't take himself."

Coaching differs from other forms of professional development or mentorship in several key ways:

- Client-Centred: The focus is on the coachee's agenda, needs, and

goals, with the coach acting as a facilitator, not an authority.
- *Solution-Oriented: Emphasizes actionable strategies and forward momentum rather than dwelling on past challenges.*
- *Empowerment: Builds the coachee's capacity to solve problems and make decisions independently.*
- *Confidential and Non-Judgmental: Provides a safe space for exploration, reflection, and growth.*

The benefits of coaching are multifaceted:

- *Clarity and Focus: Gain a clear understanding of priorities and create a roadmap for success.*
- *Skill Development: Enhance specific skills such as communication, leadership, or time management.*
- *Improved Confidence: Build self-assurance in tackling challenges and seizing opportunities.*
- *Sustainable Progress: Develop habits and strategies for long-term personal and professional growth.*

As Michael Josephson aptly noted, "A good coach improves your game. A great coach improves your life."

Coaching is for anyone seeking growth, whether they're executives looking to refine their leadership style, professionals navigating career changes, or individuals seeking balance and fulfillment in their lives.

Through curiosity, empathy, and structured support, coaching opens doors to new possibilities and empowers individuals to achieve their fullest potential. Embarking on a coaching journey can lead to profound personal and professional transformation.

In the realm of coaching, various models provide structured frameworks to guide the coaching process, ensuring that both the coach and coachee engage in a systematic and effective journey toward achieving goals. One of the most widely recognized and utilized models is the GROW model.

The GROW Model

Developed in the late 1980s by Sir John Whitmore and his colleagues, the GROW model offers a straightforward yet powerful framework for goal setting and problem-solving within coaching sessions. The acronym GROW stands for:

1. *Goal: Define what the coachee wants to achieve. This involves setting clear, specific, and attainable objectives. Questions to consider include:*

- *What do you want to accomplish in this session?*
- *What are your long-term aspirations?*

2. Reality: Examine the current situation to understand the context and identify any obstacles. This step involves honest assessment and reflection. Questions to consider include:

- *What is happening now?*
- *What challenges have you encountered?*

3. Options: Explore the possible strategies and courses of action available to achieve the goal. This encourages creative thinking and the consideration of various alternatives. Questions to consider include:

- *What are the different ways you could approach this?*
- *What resources are available to you?*

4. Will: Commit to specific actions that will be taken to move toward the goal. This step focuses on decision-making and planning. Questions to consider include:

- *What steps will you take next?*
- *When will you start?*

The GROW model's simplicity and versatility make it applicable across various coaching scenarios, from executive coaching to personal development. It facilitates a structured conversation that helps coachee gain clarity, assess their current situation, explore possibilities, and commit to actionable steps.

By integrating the GROW model into the coaching process, coaches can effectively guide their clients through a journey of self-discovery and goal attainment, fostering both personal and professional growth.

2

Understanding the Coachee

Effective coaching begins with thorough preparation, setting the stage for meaningful and productive sessions. As the legendary basketball coach John Wooden once said, "Failing to prepare is preparing to fail." This chapter delves into the essential steps a coach should undertake during the preparation phase to ensure a successful coaching engagement.

1. Understanding the Coachee

Prior to the initial session, it's crucial to gather comprehensive information about the coachee. This involves:

- *Reviewing Background Information: Examine the coachee's professional history, current role, and any prior assessments or feedback. This context aids in tailoring the coaching approach to their specific needs.*
- *Identifying Goals and Objectives: Engage the coachee in discussions to clarify their aspirations and what they aim to*

achieve through coaching. This alignment ensures that both coach and coachee are working towards common objectives.

By thoroughly understanding the coachee's background and goals, the coach can design sessions that are relevant and impactful.

2. Establishing the Coaching Agreement

A clear coaching agreement sets the foundation for the coaching relationship. Key components include:

- *Defining Roles and Responsibilities: Clarify the expectations from both the coach and the coachee, ensuring mutual understanding of each party's role in the process.*
- *Setting Boundaries and Confidentiality: Discuss the limits of the coaching relationship and emphasize the importance of confidentiality to build trust. As noted by Hoolr Coaching, "A coaching agreement is the bedrock of a fruitful coaching relationship, setting clear expectations and building trust."*
- *Agreeing on Logistics: Determine the frequency, duration, and mode of sessions (e.g., in-person, virtual) to establish a consistent structure.*

A well-defined coaching agreement fosters a transparent and trusting relationship, essential for effective coaching.

3. Preparing the Coaching Environment

The environment in which coaching takes place can significantly impact its effectiveness. Considerations include:

- *Choosing an Appropriate Setting: Select a quiet, comfortable, and private space free from distractions to facilitate open communication.*
- *Ensuring Technical Readiness: For virtual sessions, verify that all technological tools are functioning properly to prevent disruptions.*
- *Organizing Materials: Prepare any necessary documents, assessments, or resources in advance to ensure a smooth session flow.*

An optimal coaching environment enhances focus and engagement, contributing to the success of the sessions.

4. Self-Preparation of the Coach

- *The coach's readiness is pivotal to the coaching process. This involves:*
- *Reflecting on Personal Biases: Acknowledge and set aside any personal biases to approach the coachee's situation with an open mind.*
- *Enhancing Active Listening Skills: Commit to fully engaging with the coachee's narratives, ensuring they feel heard and understood. As Ralph G. Nichols emphasized, "The most basic of all human needs is the need to understand and be understood. The best way to understand people is to listen to them."*
- *Planning the Session Structure: Outline the session's agenda, including key topics to cover and questions to explore, while remaining flexible to adapt as needed.*

A coach's self-preparation ensures they are present and fully equipped to guide the coachee effectively.

5. Utilizing Assessment Tools

Assessment tools can provide valuable insights into the coachee's personality, strengths, and areas for development. Steps include:

- *Selecting Appropriate Assessments: Choose tools that align with the coachee's goals and the coaching objectives.*
- *Interpreting Results Collaboratively: Discuss the outcomes with the coachee to co-create an understanding and identify actionable steps.*

Integrating assessment tools enriches the coaching process by offering deeper insights and facilitating targeted development.

In summary, the preparation phase is a critical component of the coaching process. By diligently preparing,

coaches set the groundwork for a productive and transformative coaching journey, ultimately

empowering coachees to achieve their desired outcomes.

3

Activity

Coaching Needs Questionnaire

Please complete this form to help identify your personal objectives for coaching. Your responses will guide us in tailoring a program to meet your needs.

Personal Information

- Name: _____
- Work Address: _____
- Job Title/Role: _____
- Specific Remit within the Organization: _____

Understanding Your Strengths and Challenges

- How would you describe your top strengths? (E.g., communication, innovation, leadership)

- Which areas of your work would you like to improve or be more effective in? (E.g., data analysis, leadership skills, process management)

- If you have received feedback about your working or leadership style, what have you learned from it?

- What leadership or operational challenges do you currently face in your role? (E.g., resource limitations, cross-departmental coordination)

ACTIVITY

Coaching Needs and Objectives

- What are your top three priorities for coaching?
- What specific outcomes would you like to achieve in each priority area? (E.g., develop a project management plan, improve public speaking, build stronger networks)

Priority 1:
　Success Criteria
　Priority 2:
　Success Criteria:

Skill Development

1. Are there specific skills or knowledge areas you'd like to develop through coaching? (E.g., Excel data analysis, project leadership, stakeholder management)

2. Do you have any projects or roles in mind where these skills will be applied?

Support Needs

- Are there any resources or support systems you require to achieve your goals? (E.g., access to training, mentoring, additional tools)

2. What assistance or accommodations can we provide to ensure your coaching experience is effective?

Additional Information

- Would you like to address any other challenges or opportunities during coaching sessions?

4

Structuring Effective Coaching Sessions

A well-structured coaching session provides clarity and direction, ensuring that both coach and coachee remain focused on achieving the desired outcomes. The following components are essential for an effective coaching session:

1.Introduction and Rapport Building (5-10 minutes)

Begin by establishing a welcoming atmosphere to foster trust and open communication. This can involve casual conversation to ease into the session and a brief overview of the agenda. As noted by the Coach Foundation, "Start with a positive interaction to foster an open, communicative atmosphere."

2. Review of Previous Actions and Progress (10-15 minutes)

Discuss the coachee's progress since the last session, celebrating successes and addressing any challenges encountered. This reflection reinforces accountability and continuous improvement. According to Simply.Coach, "Reflect on any progress made since the last session, creating a sense of continuity and motivation."

3. Setting the Session's Objective (5-10 minutes)

Collaboratively identify specific goals for the current session, ensuring alignment with the coachee's overarching objectives. Clear goal-setting provides direction and purpose. As highlighted by Luisa Zhou, "Establish your goal for your session."

4. Exploration and Insight Development (20-30 minutes)

Delve into the coachee's challenges and opportunities using targeted questions and coaching techniques. This phase aims to uncover insights and foster self-awareness. The International Coach Academy emphasizes that "Each coaching session is unique… impacted by the quality of the relationship; the context of the client's challenge(s) and the individual traits of both the coach and the client that day."

5. Action Planning (10-15 minutes)

Develop actionable steps that the coachee will undertake before the next session. Ensure these actions are specific, measurable, and attainable. As per the Coach Foundation, "This segment is key for motivating the client and reaffirming their efforts and achievements."

6. Summary and Closing (5 minutes)

Recap the key points discussed, confirm the agreed-upon actions, and address any final questions. This closure reinforces commitment and clarity moving forward.

By adhering to this structure, coaches can facilitate sessions that are both efficient and impactful, fostering a productive coaching relationship.

Communication is an essential part of a coaching session. Effective communication is the cornerstone of successful coaching sessions, facilitating trust, clarity, and meaningful progress. Integrating robust communication skills and models into coaching practices enhances the coach-coachee relationship and ensures that sessions are productive and goal-oriented.

1. Active Listening

Active listening involves fully concentrating on the speaker, genuinely understanding their message, and responding thoughtfully. This skill is vital in coaching, as it ensures that the coachee feels heard and valued. Key components include:

- Maintaining Eye Contact: Demonstrates engagement and

interest.
- Avoiding Interruptions: Allows the coachee to express their thoughts completely.
- Reflecting and Paraphrasing: Ensures accurate understanding and shows empathy.

Developing active listening skills can be achieved through practice and self-awareness. Engaging in exercises that focus on withholding judgment and fully engaging with the speaker can enhance this skill.

2. The Four-Sides Model

Developed by Friedemann Schulz von Thun, the Four-Sides Model posits that every message has four facets:

Fact: The information conveyed.

Self-Revelation: What the speaker reveals about themselves.

Relationship: What the speaker thinks about the listener and their relationship.

Appeal: What the speaker wants the listener to do.

Understanding these facets helps coaches interpret messages more comprehensively, leading to more effective communication.

3. Non-Verbal Communication

Non-verbal cues, such as body language, facial expressions, and tone of voice, play a significant role in communication. Coaches should be attuned to these signals to fully understand the coachee's messages and emotions. For instance, maintaining open body language and appropriate eye contact can foster a more trusting and open coaching environment.

4. Empathy

Empathy involves understanding and sharing the feelings of another. In coaching, demonstrating empathy helps build rapport and trust, enabling coachees to feel supported and understood. This can be achieved by actively listening, validating the coachee's experiences, and responding with compassion.

5. The CLEAR Model

Developed by Peter Hawkins, the CLEAR Model emphasizes effective communication throughout the coaching process. It consists of:

Contracting: Establishing the coaching relationship and setting expectations.

Listening: Engaging in active listening to understand the coachee's perspective.

Exploring: Delving deeper into issues to uncover underlying factors.

Action: Developing actionable steps toward goals.

Review: Reflecting on progress and outcomes.

This model provides a structured approach to coaching conversations, ensuring clarity and effectiveness.

By integrating these communication skills and models into coaching sessions, coaches can enhance their effectiveness, foster stronger relationships with coachees, and facilitate meaningful progress toward the coachee's goals.

5

Implementing Effective Coaching Techniques and Tools

Employing a variety of coaching techniques and tools can enhance the coaching process, catering to the unique needs of each coachee. Some effective methods include:

1. The Wheel of Life

This tool helps coachees assess their satisfaction across different life domains, identifying areas for improvement. Evercoach describes it as "a powerful visual tool that provides clients with a 'bird's eye' view of their current life balance."

2. SMART Goal Setting

Encourages the creation of goals that are Specific, Measurable, Achievable, Relevant, and Time-bound, enhancing clarity and attainability. As noted by Lovely Impact, "SMART goals provide clarity, focus, and motivation for achieving objectives."

3. Journaling Exercises

Promotes self-reflection and deeper insight into thoughts and behaviors, facilitating personal growth. Evercoach suggests that "there are many journaling techniques you can use in your coaching practice to help clients gain clarity and insight."

4. Mindfulness and Centering Techniques

Assist coachees in becoming present and focused, reducing stress and enhancing decision-making capabilities. PositivePsychology.com highlights that "centering, breathing, or relaxation exercises can help bring both the coach and the client into a present and focused state of mind."

Employing a variety of coaching techniques and tools can enhance the coaching process, catering to the unique needs of each coachee. Some effective methods include:

5. Powerful Questioning

Utilizing open-ended questions to challenge assumptions and encourage deeper thinking. The Coaching Tools Company emphasizes "the art of asking powerful questions to help clients brainstorm ideas, explore possibilities or get to know themselves."

Integrating these techniques thoughtfully can lead to significant breakthroughs and sustained progress for coachees.

Tailoring coaching sessions to align with a coachee's unique personality enhances engagement and effectiveness. By employing specific assessment tools and adapting coaching techniques, coaches can create bespoke sessions that resonate with individual coachees.

1. Utilizing Personality Assessment Tools

Implementing personality assessments provides valuable insights into a coachee's traits, preferences, and behaviours, enabling the customization of coaching strategies. Notable tools include:

Myers-Briggs Type Indicator (MBTI): Identifies personality types based on preferences in perception and judgment, offering a framework to tailor communication and coaching approaches. For example, understanding whether a coachee is introverted or extroverted can inform the coach's strategy in facilitating discussions.

DISC Assessment: Evaluates behavioural styles across four dimensions—Dominance, Influence, Steadiness, and Conscientiousness—allowing coaches to adapt their methods to align with the coachee's natural tendencies. For instance, a coachee with a high Dominance style may prefer a direct and results-oriented approach

Hogan Personality Inventory (HPI): Assesses normal personality characteristics that influence work performance, aiding in the development of tailored coaching plans that address specific workplace behaviors. This can be particularly useful in leadership coaching to enhance interpersonal effectiveness.

Employing these tools enables coaches to design sessions that resonate with the coachee's inherent personality, fostering a more personalized and effective coaching experience.

2. Adapting Coaching Techniques to Personality Types

Recognizing and adapting to different personality types ensures that coaching techniques are effective and meaningful. Strategies include:

Matching Communication Styles: Aligning the coaching communication style with the coachee's preferences enhances understanding and rapport. For example, a coachee who prefers detailed information benefits from comprehensive explanations, while a big-picture thinker appreciates concise overviews.

Flexibility in Coaching Styles: Employing various coaching styles, such as democratic, holistic, or autocratic, based on the coachee's personality, can lead to more effective outcomes. For instance, a democratic style may engage coachees who value collaboration, while a more directive approach might suit those who prefer clear guidance.

Setting Personalized Goals: Collaboratively establishing goals that align with the coachee's values and motivations increases commitment and relevance. Understanding a coachee's personality helps in setting objectives that are both challenging and attainable, fostering sustained engagement

By customizing coaching techniques to align with individual personalities, coaches can create a supportive environment that encourages growth and development.

3. Integrating Neuro-Linguistic Programming (NLP) Techniques

NLP offers tools for understanding and influencing thought patterns and behaviours, which can be tailored to individual personalities. Techniques include:

- Mirroring and Matching: Subtly reflecting the coachee's body language and speech patterns to build rapport and trust. This approach fosters a sense of connection and understanding, making the coachee feel more comfortable and open.
- Anchoring Positive States: Helping coachees associate specific physical actions with positive emotional states, enabling them to access these states when needed. This technique can be particularly beneficial for coachees looking to manage stress or enhance confidence.

Applying NLP techniques allows coaches to tailor interventions that resonate with the coachee's unique cognitive and emotional patterns, enhancing the effectiveness of the coaching process.

Incorporating these personalized coaching techniques and tools ensures that each session is bespoke, addressing the coachee's individual personality and fostering a more impactful coaching experience.

6

Reflection and Feedback in the Coaching Process

Continuous reflection and feedback are vital for the growth of both the coachee and the coach. They ensure that the coaching process remains dynamic and responsive to the coachee's evolving needs.

1. Encouraging Self-Reflection

Prompting coachees to reflect on their experiences fosters self-awareness and personal development. As noted by PositivePsychology.com, "writing a coaching plan is critical for maintaining and documenting the progress of your coaching sessions."

2. Providing Constructive Feedback

Offering timely and specific feedback helps coachees recognize their progress and identify areas for improvement. The International Coaching Federation suggests "using coaching tools and exercises to help clients grow, build confidence and save much needed time."

3. Seeking Feedback as a Coach

Regularly soliciting feedback from coachees allows coaches to refine their methods and enhance the coaching relationship. As highlighted by Forbes,

Reflective practice is a cornerstone of effective coaching, enabling coaches to continually assess and enhance their methods. By engaging in structured reflection, coaches can gain deeper insights into their practices, leading to improved outcomes for their clients. Several models facilitate this reflective process, each offering unique approaches to self-examination and professional growth.

1. Schön's Model: Reflection-in-Action and Reflection-on-Action

Donald Schön introduced two pivotal concepts in reflective practice:

- Reflection-in-Action: This involves thinking on one's feet during the coaching session, allowing for immediate adjustments to strategies as situations unfold. It requires the coach to be aware of their actions and their effects in real-time, facilitating dynamic and responsive coaching.
- Reflection-on-Action: This occurs after the coaching session, where the coach reviews and analyzes their actions and decisions to understand what worked well and what could be improved. This post-session reflection is crucial

for long-term development and learning.

By integrating both forms of reflection, coaches can develop a more responsive and adaptive practice.

2. Rolfe's Framework for Reflective Practice

Gary Rolfe and colleagues proposed a straightforward model based on three questions:

- What?: Describing the situation or experience in detail.
- So What?: Analyzing the significance of the experience and understanding the underlying principles or lessons.
- Now What?: Determining the actions to take in response to the insights gained, planning how to apply this new understanding in future situations.

This model encourages a systematic approach to reflection, guiding coaches from mere description to actionable outcomes.

3. Gibbs' Reflective Cycle

Graham Gibbs developed a cyclical model comprising six stages:

- Description: Detailing the event or activity.
- Feelings: Discussing emotions and thoughts during the event.
- Evaluation: Assessing what was successful and what was not.
- Analysis: Understanding the situation and identifying

patterns or themes.
- Conclusion: Determining what could have been done differently.
- Action Plan: Planning specific steps for improvement in future similar situations.

Gibbs' model promotes continuous learning and development, encouraging coaches to apply their reflections to practice.

4. Kolb's Experiential Learning Cycle

David Kolb's model emphasizes learning through experience and consists of four stages:

- Concrete Experience: Engaging in a new experience or encountering a new situation.
- Reflective Observation: Reflecting on the experience from various perspectives.
- Abstract Conceptualization: Formulating theories or generalizations based on the reflections.
- Active Experimentation: Applying the new concepts in practice to test their validity.

This cycle underscores the importance of reflection in transforming experiences into actionable knowledge.

5. Borton's Developmental Framework

Terry Borton's model, which inspired Rolfe's framework, involves three simple questions:

- What?: Identifying and describing the experience.
- So What?: Understanding the implications and significance of the experience.
- Now What?: Deciding on the actions to take based on the new understanding.

This model provides a straightforward approach to reflection, facilitating quick yet effective self-assessment.

Incorporating these reflective models into coaching practice enables coaches to critically assess their methods, understand their impact, and make informed adjustments. Regular engagement in reflective practice not only enhances coaching effectiveness but also contributes to the coach's professional development and lifelong learning.

Illustrative Case: Enhancing Coaching Through Reflection

Consider the experience of a coach working with a client who struggled with public speaking anxiety. Initially, the coach employed standard techniques such as breathing exercises and visualization. However, progress was limited. Engaging in Reflection-on-Action, the coach reviewed the sessions and recognized a pattern: the client exhibited heightened anxiety when discussing past negative speaking experiences.

Utilizing Rolfe's Framework:

- What?: The client became visibly anxious when recalling previous public speaking events.
- So What?: This indicated that past experiences were a significant trigger for current anxiety, suggesting that

addressing these memories could be crucial.
- Now What?: The coach decided to incorporate techniques aimed at reframing past negative experiences, such as cognitive restructuring.

Implementing this new approach led to significant improvements. The client began to view past experiences differently, reducing anxiety levels and enhancing public speaking performance. This case exemplifies how reflective practice enables coaches to adapt strategies to meet clients' specific needs effectively.

By consistently applying reflective models, coaches can refine their approaches, leading to more personalized and successful coaching outcomes.

7

Contact Us.

CONTACT US.

Website : *www.wednesdayswithjames.com*

Email : *wednesdayswithjames@gmail.com*

Youtube : *@wednesdaysWJ*

8

References

- *Whitmore, J. (2010). Coaching for Performance: GROWing Human Potential and Purpose: The Principles and Practice of Coaching and Leadership. Nicholas Brealey Publishing.*
- *Google Books*
- *McCartney, B. (n.d.). Quote*
- *Josephson, M. (n.d.). Quote*

www.ingramcontent.com/pod-product-compliance
Lightning Source LLC
Chambersburg PA
CBHW031929240526
45464CB00023B/2880